EXTREME SPORTS BIOGRAPHIES

DANNY HARF
Wakeboarding Champion

Ian F. Mahaney

The Rosen Publishing Group's
PowerKids Press™
New York

To my favorite niece, Claire

Safety gear, including buoyancy vests, helmets, and gloves, should be worn while wakeboarding. Do not attempt tricks without proper gear, instruction, and supervision.

Published in 2005 by The Rosen Publishing Group, Inc.
29 East 21st Street, New York, NY 10010

First Edition

Editor: Heidi Leigh Johansen
Book Design: Mike Donnellan
Photo Researcher: Peter Tomlinson

Photo Credits: Cover © Reuters NewMedia Inc./CORBIS; pp. 4, 7 (left), 8, 16 Icon Sports Media; pp. 4 (inset), 12, 15, 20, 22 Tony Donaldson/Icon SMI; pp. 7 (right), 19 Mike Isler/Icon SMI; p. 11 (left) AP Photo/H. Rumph, Jr.; p. 11 (right) © Al Fuchs/NewSport/CORBIS; p. 19 (inset) AP Photo/Chris Polk.

Library of Congress Cataloging-in-Publication Data

Mahaney, Ian F.
Danny Harf : wakeboarding champion / Ian F. Mahaney.
     p. cm. — (Extreme sports biographies)
Summary: Details the life and successes of professional wakeboarder Danny Harf, who won three straight X Games gold medals by 2003. Includes bibliographical references and index.
ISBN 1-4042-2743-1 (Library Binding)
1. Harf, Danny—Juvenile literature. 2. Wakeboarders—California—Biography—Juvenile literature. [1. Harf, Danny. 2. Wakeboarders.] I. Title. II. Series.

GV838.H364M35 2005
796.04'6—dc22

                                    2003020950

Manufactured in the United States of America

Contents

Danny Harf rides the wake on his wakeboard while holding on to a sturdy towrope. Danny needs to be strong and fit to be one of the best wakeboarders in the world.

Extreme Wakeboarding

Wakeboarding is an **extreme sport** that was invented in the 1980s. **Surfers** noticed that they could ride the waves made by boats. A wave that trails a boat is called a **wake**. The surfers soon thought of a new way to ride a wake. They secured boards to their feet and held on to a rope **attached** to the boat, called a towrope. They used the wake to **perform** tricks, such as spinning or flipping. **Professional** wakeboarders often perform tricks using **obstacles** on a wakeboarding course. Some of the obstacles on the course include a kicker and a slider. A professional wakeboarder is an **expert** who earns a living wakeboarding. One of the top wakeboarding **champions** today is Danny Harf. Danny has been wakeboarding since he was about 12 years old. With stars like Danny, wakeboarding has become a popular extreme sport.

Getting to Know Danny Harf

Danny Harf is a professional, or pro, wakeboarder. He was born on October 15, 1984, in Visalia, California. Danny's parents, Daniel and Diana, often travel with Danny to wakeboarding **competitions**. Before Danny began wakeboarding, Danny's father taught Danny how to surf in the ocean. Danny's family moved to a house on a lake near Orlando, Florida, in 1996. Danny and his sister, Lauren, began to wakeboard. Danny and Lauren became very good wakeboarders because they had plenty of opportunities to practice. Lauren is also a professional wakeboarder. She competes against other women wakeboarders in many of the same competitions in which Danny competes. Danny trains with other wakeboarders in Florida and practices his flips and spins on a **trampoline** to increase his strength and **flexibility**.

Danny is a "goofy-footer," meaning he wakeboards with his right foot forward. Danny's sister, Lauren, is an accomplished wakeboarder as well. Lauren often competes against wakeboarders Emily Copeland and Dallas Friday.

Wakeboarding is the fastest-growing water sport in the United States. As many as 2 million people worldwide have tried wakeboarding. Above: Danny performs a spinning trick off the wake while holding on to the towrope with only his right hand.

Danny's a Star

In 1999, Danny Harf was already recognized as a wakeboarder who could perform many **difficult** tricks, while making the tricks look easy. That year Danny competed in the U.S. Junior **Series**, which is a wakeboard tour. A wakeboard tour is a competition of several wakeboarding events that are held in different places throughout the summer. The locations that the tour visits in the summer are called tour stops. The U.S. Junior Series is a wakeboard tour that is limited to skilled wakeboarders who are 18 years old and younger. That summer Danny's hard work and practice paid off. Winning the gold **medal** with a strong wakeboarding **performance**, Danny became the 1999 U.S. Junior Series champion. That means that Danny was the best wakeboarder in the United States under 19 years old.

Soon Danny Harf was skilled enough at wakeboarding to begin competing professionally. Danny competed in the Pro Wakeboard Tour in 2000. Danny competed in the top level of the Pro Wakeboard Tour, against some of the best wakeboarders in the country, including Parks Bonifay and Shaun Murray. As is the U.S. Junior Series, the Pro Wakeboard Tour is held in several locations. Danny won one Pro Wakeboard Tour event in 2000, in Oklahoma City. Danny also came in sixth place at the X Games that year. The X Games is an extreme sports competition held every year. In-line skating, motocross, wakeboarding, and skateboarding are examples of X-Games events. The very first X-Games wakeboarding event was held in 1996. Danny did so well in his **rookie** year, or his first professional year, that he was named Rookie of the Year in 2000.

Left: The very first X Games was held in 1995. That year it was called the Extreme Games. In 1996, the wakeboarding event was added. It is now a very popular X-Games event. Right: Danny performs a trick using the wake.

Danny Harf greets his fans after a successful competition. Danny and other wakeboarding superstars often sign their names on fans' wakeboards. Young wakeboarders look up to Danny and copy his moves.

A Big Win at the X Games

Danny Harf had an even better year as a professional wakeboarder in 2001. The 2001 X Games was held in Philadelphia, Pennsylvania. The best extreme sports **athletes** in the country took part. Some people believe that the 2001 X Games had some of the best wakeboarding performances in the history of the X Games. Sixteen-year-old Danny took home the 2001 X-Games gold medal with his bold wakeboarding moves. Danny finally joined the top group of wakeboarders, which included Darin Shapiro. Darin had won the X-Games wakeboarding event in 2000 and in 1998. Danny Harf was becoming popular with wakeboarding fans. In a **poll** of readers of *Wake Boarding* magazine, he was voted the fifth-most-popular **contestant** in the sport. *Wake Boarding* magazine is a popular magazine among wakeboarding fans.

Taking It Easy and Winning Again

Even professional wakeboarders like Danny Harf can hurt themselves. Some of the moves that wakeboarders perform, as well as the obstacles that they face in competition, can be tricky and difficult. That is why wakeboarders use helmets and life jackets. In 2002, Danny hurt his right knee on an obstacle known as a kicker. Danny Harf missed many Pro Wakeboard Tour events in the summer of 2002 because he had to rest his knee. When Danny went to Philadelphia for the X Games that summer, he was ready to compete. Even though Danny fell during one of his first tricks, he **amazed** his fans by getting back up and completing the rest of his tricks perfectly. At the age of 17, Danny won the gold medal at the X Games, one of the most important wakeboarding events in the country, for the second time.

Danny performs a trick using an obstacle called a slider. He slides along the top of the slider, then he jumps off. Notice that Danny has his back toward the boat in this trick. A "digger" is a hard fall off a wakeboard.

Danny performs a daring 360 in competition. One full flip in midair is called a 360, or a 360-degree flip. A 720 equals two full flips, and a 900 is two and one-half flips!

Danny's Wakeboarding Tricks

A basic wakeboarding move that many beginners perform is riding with one hand holding the towrope. A simple move that Danny mastered early is called the backscratcher. In this trick, Danny jumps into the air off the wake, and, before he lands, he bends his knees until the wakeboard comes close to his lower back and then he brings his feet down again.

One of Danny Harf's favorite tricks on a wakeboard is a mute 900. A 900 is flipping two and one-half times in the air. A mute is grabbing the wakeboard on the toeside, or the part of the board that is closest to the rider's toes. So Danny's favorite trick is spinning around two and one-half times while grabbing the board. Another fun trick that Danny performs is a whirlybird 720, in which he performs a backflip over the wake while spinning around twice.

Three-Time Champion

The year 2003 was another successful year for Danny Harf. At 18 years old, he won his third X-Games gold medal in Los Angeles, California. Danny won because he completed an amazing trick. He performed a perfect 900 followed by a whirlybird 720. One week later, Danny won a second major competition. Danny scored the gold medal at the second event of the World Wakeboard Association's (WWA's) Vans Triple Crown of Wakeboarding Series. The WWA plans professional wakeboarding events and chooses judges and wakeboarders for competitions. Danny became the 2003 Vans Triple Crown champion by winning the most points in the three Triple Crown events. In the first event, Danny placed third. He also came in third place in the final Vans Triple Crown event in October 2003, right before his nineteenth birthday.

Harf won his third Men's Wakeboarding Freestyle X-Games event in 2003 with a score of 93.70. He amazed his fans and the judges with his unbelievably smooth and tricky wakeboarding moves.

Speedboats pull professional wakeboarders at speeds of up to 20 miles per hour (32 km/h). This fast speed helps wakeboarders to "catch air" and to perform tricks, such as 360-degree flips, using the wake.

Extreme Safety and Extreme Gear

Wakeboarding is an extreme, fun sport. As do all extreme athletes, wakeboarders must be extra careful when they perform. Professional wakeboarders like Danny Harf are required to wear helmets and life jackets in competitions that have obstacles. It is smart to wear a helmet and a life jacket whenever you wakeboard. Danny rides what is called a twin-tipped wakeboard. Most wakeboards today are twin-tipped. This means that the front of the wakeboard is the same as the back of the wakeboard. The wakeboard is **symmetrical** so that wakeboarders can perform tricks and land in the opposite direction than the one in which they started. Wakeboards are about 1 foot (.3 m) wide and 4 feet (1 m) long. Bindings are rubber or plastic straps that keep the board attached to wakeboarders' feet while flying through the air doing amazing tricks.

Check Out Danny on the Slider

By the time Danny Harf turned 19 years old, he had won the wakeboarding event at the X Games three years in a row. We can expect to see a lot more of Danny's inventive wakeboarding moves in the **future**. If you are interested in seeing more of Danny Harf, check out his Pointless **Posse** videos. Danny and many of his wakeboarding friends, including Parks Bonifay, Erik Ruck, Shane Bonifay, and Chad Sharpe, make these extreme wakeboarding videos. These athletes perform many of their most difficult tricks on the slider obstacle. The slider is a pipe that is about 30 feet (9 m) long, which wakeboarders use to slide on and to perform tricks. Pay attention to Danny Harf. You never know what cool trick he will come up with next!

Glossary

amazed (uh-MAYZD) Filled with wonder.

athletes (ATH-leets) People who take part in sports.

attached (uh-TACHD) Fastened.

champions (CHAM-pee-unz) The best, or the winners.

competitions (kom-pih-TIH-shinz) Games.

contestant (kun-TES-tint) A person who participates in a competition.

difficult (DIH-fih-kult) Hard to do.

expert (EK-spert) A person who is very good at an activity.

extreme sport (ek-STREEM SPORT) A bold and uncommon sport, such as BMX, in-line skating, motocross, skateboarding, snowboarding, and wakeboarding.

flexibility (flek-sih-BIH-lih-tee) An ability to move and bend in many directions.

future (FYOO-chur) The time that is coming.

medal (MEH-dul) A small, round piece of metal given as a prize.

obstacles (OB-stih-kulz) Objects that wakeboarders use to perform tricks.

perform (per-FORM) To carry out, to do.

performance (per-FOR-mens) An act, such as the riding in a wakeboarding event.

poll (POHL) A voting of opinions.

posse (PAH-see) A group of people who are interested in a certain thing.

professional (pruh-FEH-shuh-nul) Paid for what he or she does.

rookie (RU-kee) Referring to a player's first year.

series (SEER-eez) A group of games.

surfers (SERF-erz) People who use boards to ride ocean waves.

symmetrical (sih-MEH-trih-kul) Describes an object that is the same on both sides.

trampoline (tram-puh-LEEN) Cloth attached to springs used for tumbling.

wake (WAYK) The wave that follows a boat when it moves.

Index

Web Sites

Due to the changing nature of Internet links, PowerKids Press has developed an online list of Web sites related to the subject of this book. This site is updated regularly. Please use this link to access the list: www.powerkidslinks.com/esb/harf/